A Letter to My...

HEARTFELT TRIBUTES TO MOTHERS, DAUGHTERS, AND FRIENDS WHO SHAPE OUR LIVES

REAL LOVE, REAL MEMORIES, REAL CONNECTIONS

© 2024 ALL RIGHTS RESERVED.

Published by She Rises Studios Publishing **www.SheRisesStudios.com**.

No part of this book may be reproduced or transmitted in any form whatsoever, electronic, or mechanical, including photocopying, recording, or by any informational storage or retrieval system without the expressed written, dated and signed permission from the publisher and co-authors.

LIMITS OF LIABILITY/DISCLAIMER OF WARRANTY:

The co-authors and publisher of this book have used their best efforts in preparing this material. While every attempt has been made to verify the information provided in this book, neither the co-authors nor the publisher assumes any responsibility for any errors, omissions, or inaccuracies.

The co-authors and publisher make no representation or warranties with respect to the accuracy, applicability, or completeness of the contents of this book. They disclaim any warranties (expressed or implied), merchantability, or for any purpose. The co-authors and publisher shall in no event be held liable for any loss or other damages, including but not limited to special, incidental, consequential, or other damages.

ISBN: 978-1-964619-82-8

INTRODUCTION

Some words are meant to last forever.

"A Letter To My..." is more than a collection of letters—it's a celebration of the relationships that shape us, uplift us, and stay with us through all of life's journeys. In these pages, you will find heartfelt tributes to the remarkable women who have made an indelible mark on our hearts: mothers, daughters, sisters, and friends. Each letter is a deeply personal expression of love, gratitude, and connection—an enduring testament to the bonds that make us who we are.

This beautifully crafted hardcover book is organized into thoughtful sections, each focused on a different facet of these cherished relationships. Through touching words and tender reflections, you'll experience the depth of a mother's unconditional love, the pride in a daughter's accomplishments, and the steadfast support of true friendship.

More than just a keepsake, *"A Letter To My..."* serves as a reminder of what truly matters in life: the people we love, the ones who know us best, and the powerful ties that unite us across time and distance. These letters are a tribute to the power of love in all its forms, a gift that honors the connections that sustain us.

We invite you to take a moment to pause, reflect, and celebrate the extraordinary women in your life. Let these words inspire you to write your own letters of love, gratitude, and devotion to those who hold a special place in your heart.

A Letter to my... Mother

Hanna Olivas

Dear Mom,

I want to take a moment to tell you just how much I love you, cherish you, and appreciate everything you've done for me and my sister. As I sit here and reflect, my heart is filled with gratitude for the incredible woman you are and for the life lessons you've instilled in us through your strength, perseverance, and resilience.

Growing up, I didn't always fully grasp the weight of your struggles as a single mom raising two little girls. But now, as a mother myself, I look back with awe and deep respect for how hard you fought for us. You juggled so much—working tirelessly to keep yourself afloat while also being our protector, provider, and biggest cheerleader. It couldn't have been easy, but you made us feel so important and loved, even when life wasn't easy for you.

Mom, thank you for teaching me what it means to be strong and brave. You showed me how to weather life's storms and, more importantly, how to shine when the rainbows finally appear. Through your example, I've learned the value of independence and the power of faith. Your unwavering belief in God and the way you walked through life's challenges with grace have been some of the greatest lessons you've ever taught me.

Life wasn't always easy for any of us, but you always did your best. You never gave up on us, and you never gave up on yourself. That resilience—the strength to keep going even when things are tough—is something I carry with me every single day. It's a part of who I am because of you.

Mom, you have given me so much more than words can express. Your love, your faith, and your determination have shaped me into the woman I am today. I am so proud to call you my mother, and I feel incredibly blessed that God chose you for me.

Thank you for everything—for your sacrifices, your unwavering love, and your endless lessons. You've taught me not just how to survive but how to truly live with purpose and joy.

I love you more than words can ever convey.

With all my heart.

Your Oldest Daughter,
R. JoHanna Olivas

Hanna Olivas

Dear Mama Patsy,

I hope this letter brings a smile to your face because it comes straight from my heart. I want to thank you for all the extraordinary qualities you have shared with me, for the unconditional love you have shown, and for the beautiful way you have accepted me as one of your own.

From the very beginning, you made me feel like part of the family, not just as a daughter-in-law but as someone truly cherished. Your kindness, warmth, and love have always stood out to me, and I am constantly in awe of the light you bring wherever you go. When you walk into a room, your presence lights it up, and everyone around you feels the joy and peace you carry in your heart.

You are an amazing mother, mother-in-law, and grandmother to my kids and great-grandkids. Your love and support are endless, and you have become such an important part of our lives. Watching the way you care for our family, the wisdom you share, and the strength you exude has been a gift I am so grateful for.

Thank you for being a true example of grace, love, and generosity. You have shown me what it means to love unconditionally, and I am so blessed to have you in my life.

With all my love and gratitude.

Your Daughter In Love,
Hanna Olivas

Adriana Luna Carlos

Dear Mom,

As I sit down to write this letter, I find myself reflecting on the countless ways you've shaped my life and filled it with love, laughter, and lessons that I carry with me every day. You are more than my mom; you are my friend, my teacher, and the heart of so many of my happiest memories.

I'll never forget that car ride—the one where you didn't see the dip in the road. One moment, we were cruising along, and the next, we were airborne, screaming and laughing in sheer disbelief. Thankfully, we all made it out unscathed, but the laughter from that day has stayed with me forever. It's moments like these that define our relationship—moments filled with humor, spontaneity, and a shared understanding of each other's quirks. Somehow, you always know how to make me laugh, and I like to think I've inherited a bit of your incredible sense of humor.

Christmas is something we've always shared a special connection over, and it's one of the things I love most about us. You have this incredible way of turning the season into pure magic. From transforming the house into a winter wonderland to making sure every single ornament—no matter how small—finds its way onto the tree (even if we can't see the branches), you've always brought so much joy to the holidays. It's not just about the decorations; it's about the warmth and love you pour into every moment. You've shown me how to celebrate not just the season but the people around us, and that's a gift I'll always treasure.

But it's not just during the holidays that you shine. You've taught me so much about life—lessons I lean on every single day. From you, I've learned the importance of compassion and what it truly means to give with a full heart. You've shown me that forgiveness isn't just about others; it's a gift we give ourselves to move forward with peace. And, of course, the habit of rising early—it's something I used to groan about, but now, I cherish those quiet moments of productivity and reflection in the mornings, a practice that I owe entirely to you.

What I admire most about you, though, is your ability to always find the joy in life, no matter the circumstances. Your humor is endless, your heart is boundless, and your love is something I feel even when we're miles apart. I hope you know how deeply I respect and admire you for all that you are and all that you've done for our family.

As we look to the future, I want to create even more memories with you. While there's time we've lost along the way, I hope we can continue to heal, laugh, and build new traditions together. I want our family to grow and thrive, always carrying forward the values and love you've instilled in us. Whether it's more Christmas mornings surrounded by the sea of ornaments or simply more everyday moments of laughter, I'm grateful for the time we've shared and excited for what's still to come.

Thank you, Mom, for being the light in my life, the one who always knows how to make me laugh, and the person who taught me the true meaning of love and family. You are my Christmas Joy and my favorite person to laugh with. I'm so lucky to have you as my mom and I love you so much.

With all my love,
Adriana

Adriana Luna Carlos

Dear Grandma,

Even though it has been so many years since you left us, you have never left my heart. I think of you often, and your memory continues to inspire me. You were such a loving, warm presence in my life, even in the short time we shared together, and I will always cherish the beautiful moments we had.

I remember sitting next to you on the couch, watching novelas on TV, and playing Lotería. I can still picture us laughing as we ate pan dulce with milk, feeling so safe and loved just being by your side. And those nights when you comforted me to sleep—I'll never forget the warmth and care in the way you held me close. Even though I was so little, those memories are etched in my heart forever.

Grandma, you shaped me in ways I'm only now starting to fully understand. You taught me the importance of standing my ground, not by words but by the way you carried yourself—with such strength and independence. You were a small, petite woman, but to me, you felt larger than life. I looked up to you—literally and figuratively—and I still do. Your personality was so strong, yet your heart was so gentle, and that combination of strength and love is something I strive for every day.

I loved everything about you, but one thing I'll never forget is your incredible cooking. You made all the food for the family, but your homemade flour tortillas were legendary. Everyone craved them, and they were a part of what made our family meals feel so special. You brought us all together around the table, and even though I didn't fully appreciate it back then, I see now just how much love you poured into every meal.

During the holidays, I don't remember every detail, but I do remember your joy when you watched all of us grandkids opening presents. The way you looked at us—with so much love in your eyes—is a memory that still brings me comfort. You had this incredible ability to make everyone feel seen and loved, and I wish I could have had more time with you to soak in that love and learn more from your wisdom.

Grandma, I miss you so much. I've prayed to you often throughout my life, and when I was younger, I would write to you in my journal as if I were talking to you. I still believe you hear me, and I hope you know how much you mean to me. I know my life would have been different if you had lived longer, but even in the short time we had, you gave me so much. Thank you for your love, your strength, and for being there for my mom in the best way you could. It's something I will always be grateful for.

I love you and miss you, Grandma. You will always be in my heart, guiding me and reminding me of the strength and love that runs through our family.

With all my love,
Adriana

Kenya Elizabeth Aissa, MS

BEYOND THE HORIZON: A MOTHER'S LEGACY OF WANDERLUST, ADVENTURE, AND LOVE

Dear Mom,

"M is for the many things she gave me
O is for the other things she gave me
T is for the thousands of things she gave me
H is for the hundreds of things she gave me
E is for everything she gave me
R is for the rest of the stuff she gave me...
What does that spell? MOTHER! MOTHER! MOTHER!"
—Mom's Theme Song, by me

As I sit down to write this letter, I marvel at the incredible journey that is your life—a journey that is not only a testament to your resilience but also to your celebrated career excellence, your fearless drive to explore the world, and your borderline crazy determination to protect and uplift me, your only child. You have always been my guiding star, showing me that life is not just about being another cog in society's machine, but about taking on every exciting opportunity with open arms and an open heart. This letter is my tribute to you, a tribute to the remarkable woman who has shaped my understanding of adventure, love, and the boundless possibilities life has to offer.

As a child, it never occurred to me how hard your struggles were. Now that I, too, am a mom, I realize that the unwillingness to acknowledge the mental heavy lifting of motherhood is universal in our society. Your resilience was not just a skill honed from necessity, but an integral part of who you are. When faced with racism in the workplace, financial drains, and a husband who I'll delicately describe as "problematic", you never backed down; instead, you faced these challenges head-on, teaching me that every setback is merely a precursor to a comeback.

I remember all the years of you working after hours, tutoring your students, and how you shared your lunch with those who didn't have one. Your passion for scientific research at various prestigious national laboratories also had a profound effect on me. It wasn't until I was much older that I began to see how expanding my knowledge through education became a lifelong pursuit. I often describe you as a fearless but cautious seeker, and an icon, but not at all humble about it. Modesty is overrated. If you bad, you bad.

You've always encouraged me to explore new ideas, to think critically, and to never settle for mediocrity in life, relationships, or myself. You instilled in me the belief that education is the key to unlocking doors. Isn't it ironic that despite my utter loathing of science, I'm now a yoga teacher who loves anatomy? Isn't it wild that despite my deep dislike of math, as I write this, I'm sitting in a classroom where I just taught pre-algebraic equations? Life sure is strange, but I am forever grateful for the foundation you set for me.

Perhaps what I admire most about you, Mom, is your adventurous spirit, your unquenchable wanderlust that has taken you beyond the horizon to explore countless countries, cultures, food, languages, and people around the globe. No matter where you are, interesting, intelligent, dynamic people always seem to be drawn to you. You have always believed that travel is more than just visiting new places; it's about immersing yourself in different experiences and connecting with people from all walks of life. My friends joke that you're an international spy, and I'm not entirely sure they're wrong! Your stories of far-off lands, vibrant communities, sexy foreign men, and unique cuisine have painted a picture of a world full of intrigue and possibility. I love that I was only 5 years old in my first passport picture, the first of many. Traveling is one of my greatest passions. You taught me that the world is vast and beautiful, and that adventure awaits those who dare to seek it.

I remember when we traveled to Ghana, I was barely 11 years old. Upon disembarking the airplane, the heat rising from the asphalt hit me like an oven. I paused and looked back at you, then jumped onto the Motherland with both feet. Something in my young brain was aware that this was an extremely cool moment. Living in Ghana took us on a journey that neither you, me, or my godmother Karen ("Simi") could have dreamed of. From bustling cities to serene countryside, you showed me the beauty of diversity and the richness of human connection. You would engage with locals, learn their stories, and embrace their traditions, all while encouraging me to do the same. The first time I went to France, I had a long and energetic "conversation" at a party with another young woman for hours. I can't explain it, but she didn't speak English, and I didn't speak French! Still, we found a way to communicate through our limited bits of each other's language, hand gestures, and nodding encouragement to each other. It worked because you've impressed upon me that the world is a tapestry of experiences waiting to be explored, and that every interaction is a chance to learn and connect.

As I reflect on your legacy, I see the values you have instilled in me: an impenetrable resolve, a strong belief in myself and my own abilities, never-ending curiosity, and a love for adventure. Mom, thank you for being my mother, my mentor, and my greatest source of inspiration. I will cherish your legacy and pass it on to my son, godchildren, and grandchildren. I plan to embrace life with the same fervor and passion that you have always shown. My promise to you, to myself, and to any women and girls that may be inspired by me, is to always forge my own path, to get back up when I fall, and to continue to prioritize travel, adventure, and excellence.

As I look toward the horizon, I know that no matter where life takes us, I will always be grateful for the foundation you have built and the legacy you continue to create.

Your daughter,
Kennybee

Ana Martinez, RN

The Price of Love

To My Mom, I Miss You

Dear Readers,

Have you ever watched the animated movie *Coco* or listened to the song "Remember Me"? It's a beautiful, powerful song that carries a message of love and remembrance. As a motherless daughter, I can't help but cry, knowing it was the last movie I would ever watch with my mom. That makes it even more powerful, especially since the film is so deeply about family and memories. The song resonates with me on an incredibly emotional level.

Mom, I miss you so much since the day you died on December 27, 2017. You were young—only 53. It felt so unfair. I felt angry, depressed, lonely, and, most of all, kept asking why. Why you? You were such a strong, joyful woman. You never complained, even though you were working three jobs. You taught Spanish at the University of Nevada, Las Vegas, served as a domestic violence counselor, and washed pots at the Circus Circus Hotel and Casino. You worked the graveyard shift at the casino just to get health insurance—a job you disliked and that stressed you out, but one you were afraid to quit because starting over seemed impossible.

You slept so little, yet you were always calm and ready to help. You loved your granddaughter Amelia, and I'm so grateful you had the chance to enjoy the first two years of her life. Maybe you were disappointed that I got pregnant and didn't pursue higher education. But now, I believe that maybe it happened so you could experience the joy of being a grandmother.

We live as if we have all the time in the world to do the things we want to do. Had I known my mom only had a few months left to live, I believe we would have spent more time together, and I would have been on my best behavior. However, I am so grateful for the last trips we made, especially to Disneyland not knowing it would be our last family vacation, days before she was admitted to the hospital and ultimately leave us.

You'd think my experience as a hospice nurse would have helped me cope with losing her. But at that time, I had only worked in hospice admissions, so when she was in the hospital, I knew she was an ideal candidate. Yet, as her daughter, I did everything the doctors suggested—until it came down to either amputating her fingers and toes or discontinuing the ventilator and transitioning her to hospice care.

I asked the Catholic priest to come to provide the sacrament of the Last Rites. Despite the ventilator, she was awake and declined the sacrament. My aunt and I had to sit with her and explain her medical situation before she accepted it the next day. I was only 26, making these decisions. She understood, and we made arrangements. After eight days in the hospital, her ventilator was discontinued, and she was transferred to hospice, where she died surrounded by the people who loved her, without pain, about 24 hours later.

Mom, I am so grateful that our family and close friends could be with you during those days and final hours. I hope you could feel how deeply you were loved by all of us. My only regret is that Amelia didn't get the chance to say goodbye. You babysat her on a Saturday night, and then by Monday, you were in the hospital. I know you didn't want her to see you like that, and I honored your wish, but part of me feels it would have been better for her to say goodbye.

For days and months afterward, every time someone came home, she would ask and look for you. These memories hurt so much, and I'm crying as I write them down.

So, how do we cope with the loss of a loved one—someone who was close to you and loved you unconditionally? Grief looks different for everyone; there is no standard pattern, timeline, or 'normal' way to grieve. While there are five commonly recognized stages (denial, anger, bargaining, depression, and acceptance), grief is not linear, and we don't simply 'get over it.' Instead, grief comes in waves, rising and falling, sometimes overlapping or circling back.

Have you heard of the 'ball and the box' analogy? It helped me understand my grief. In the beginning, the ball—which represents grief—is large, taking up most of the space in the box, which represents life. It hits the pain button constantly. But as time goes on, the ball gradually gets smaller, hitting the pain button less and less. This change allows us time to recover between moments of pain, though those moments can be just as intense.

This analogy explains why, even years later, the pain can feel just as strong. A certain smell, sound, or a glimpse of something that reminds you of your loved one can still bring back flashes of anger, a pang of 'what if' thoughts, and waves of sadness. But alongside all of that, you also feel a quiet sense of peace—a gentle acceptance that has grown over time.

Mom, the first stage—denial—hit me hard and fast. In those initial days, I couldn't fully grasp that you were really gone. My mind played tricks on me, convincing me that maybe this was all a bad dream. I remember thinking that you must just be at work, or sleeping, which was why you weren't calling or answering the phone. This denial wasn't about pretending you hadn't died; it was that my mind refused to accept the permanence of your absence. I felt so lonely. I had never wanted a sibling, but for the first time, I wished I had one.

Then came anger, which was probably the hardest for me to face because I was angry—at you, Mom, at the doctors, and especially at myself for not acting quickly enough. As a nurse, I felt like I had failed you. It was like trying to lash out at something invisible. Over time, I realized that anger was my way of trying to regain control over something uncontrollable. It was a surface emotion; underneath it, I was actually heartbroken. Letting go of the anger took time. It wasn't until I went through your belongings that I began to understand you more deeply, finding empathy and a little acceptance.

Bargaining was quieter, more private—a series of 'if only' statements. If only I'd spent more time with you. If only we'd had that last conversation. Did I hug you enough? Did I show you I loved you enough? I would lie awake at night, going through endless scenarios in my mind, searching for some way I could change the outcome, some alternate timeline where you were still here. I even wished for you to appear to me as a ghost, to answer my questions. Did you know you were sick? Why did you refuse to see a doctor in Mexico when your friend offered to take you? My deepest desire was, and still is, to feel close to you, to find some last chance of connecting. When I dream of you, that's when I feel closest to you. When I visit Disneyland or go on a cruise, I feel you with me.

Depression was probably the longest and heaviest stage. I didn't have the luxury of lying in bed. As your only daughter, I had to handle all of your affairs, from your belongings to the paperwork and funeral arrangements. I had asked you to prepare a power of attorney and living will, but you hadn't, saying you didn't have anything significant to pass on and that I was your only daughter anyway. Sorting through your financial situation was overwhelming. I was also completing a divorce, learning how to co-parent, and caring for my own daughter. I remember feeling guilty for laughing or smiling, as though enjoying anything was a betrayal of you. Counseling didn't help much at first, because this pain required me to confront not just your loss but also the parts of myself that had changed because of it.

Acceptance crept in gradually. Over time, I began to feel moments of peace, accepting that your absence was now a part of my story, a part of who I am. I began to notice the ways you live on in me. Acceptance didn't erase the pain, but it allowed me to carry your memory in a way that felt lighter. I learned that acceptance is about moving forward.

Grieving isn't something you finish or complete; it's something you carry. My mother's absence is a part of me—woven into the way I live each day. I believe that's what grief ultimately taught me. It's a way of holding onto love, of honoring the people who shaped us, even after they're gone. Grief is the price we pay for loving someone.

I want to honor and remember my mom by encouraging you, dear readers, to live your best lives. The most precious thing we have is time, and we never know how much we truly have. In *The Voices of 100 Women* and *Sensual Symphony*, I outline practical steps to take toward living your best life. Please call your mom for me and tell her you love her.

With all my love and gratitude,

Ana Lucia

Sandra Dawe

Mom,

The hardest part about being the most consistent person in someone's life is that you get blamed for everything that goes wrong. You were my consistent one. And I am so sorry that I blamed you for anything that ever went wrong in my life because all of the trials and tribulations led me to the amazing life I have today. While I am sorry for being the biggest jerk of a daughter sometimes, I am also thankful that you gave me the freedom to be a strong-willed, determined rebel. I've never fully understood why I was so angry, so I could never tell you, but I want to try to explain it now.

Anger as Fear

I didn't understand fear until I was an adult when I was filled with so many hopes and dreams, but at times, I would find myself paralyzed with fear instead of moving forward with confidence. It would stop me in my tracks and knock me over with no one to blame. Fear took my breath away and, at times, called out to me in the middle of the night, waking me from my sleep. I had no one to yell at but myself.

By the time I was 14, I was so consumed with fear that I would lash out at every chance I got. I was scared I wouldn't make friends at my new schools, but today I am incredibly thankful for how easily I make friends and for a heart that calls out to those who are different or left out.

I feared failure, but now my life is filled with stories of success. I feared that you would stop loving me or leave me the way my dad did, but no matter how mean I was, you would just keep showing up. You took those moments when I knew you just wanted to scream at me, and instead, you stood your ground and showed me true love. Your consistency is what helped me continue to show up for myself, for my own children, and for those around me. I am thankful that you are consistent.

Anger as Confusion

I was a teenager when I realized that you were also a teenager when you gave birth to me. I can't imagine what it was like to become a mother instead of getting to go to high school. I spent years wondering how my life held you back, wondering why I was brought to this earth anyway, or even worse, wishing I had never been born. This created so much confusion and anger for me. I hated that I was mad all the time, but I had no idea why I felt these things or how to control those feelings. These feelings overwhelmed me and led to me lashing out in rebellion.

Most of the time, I focused on what was missing instead of what we had. We didn't always have as much money as we needed, but we always had fun. You gave me many gifts along the way. You gave me a bonus dad who loves me, a baby brother and sister to mentor, but you also gave me my childhood best friend. Despite moving out of state shortly after meeting her, you made sure we were pen pals and stayed connected. As soon as we moved back home, you would surprise me by picking her up so she could spend the weekend with us. You did the work for us even when we grew apart in high school until she and I could sustain our friendship on our own as adults. I think about all the memories you created that we still cherish and how those memories created the women we are today.

When we were just eight, we treated my new baby brother and sister like our personal baby dolls, changing their clothes and keeping them entertained. When we were ten, you took us to the skating rink and let us skate and laugh for hours. At twelve, I got grounded for a weekend and it was her that gave me my first romance novel, which was extremely inappropriate, but it led to my lifelong love of reading. When we were fourteen, she got to come camping with us, and during that trip, we both got our first summer crush kiss! She was there for the death of many family members and the birth of all my children. All of my best stories start and end with our adventures, and we are still friends today because of you. While I spent many nights crying myself to sleep in confusion or what felt unfair, I did not see the lifetime of lessons or what I was learning about friendship and sisterhood growing into the shade tree that still provides comfort for me today. Thank you for filling in the gaps to give me life's greatest gift—Life and Love.

From Anger to Gratitude

When I finally became an adult and a mother, a new understanding of your love for me was formed. I finally could see with clear eyes and a grateful heart. I am not angry anymore and haven't been for many, many years now. Some days I look into the mirror and see you staring back at me. I see the determination in my eyes that came from watching you create everything from nothing. I see the courage that I saw in you when you had no idea how a situation would turn out, but you never gave up. I find myself on my knees in prayer because while we didn't always agree on religion, you showed me how to love Jesus as well as the power and miracles that prayer could bring. This life has brought me more miracles than I could ever imagine, and I know it is because you have been my biggest cheerleader and prayer warrior.

There is one thing I know, you were chosen to be my mom with a purpose, and I want you to know that I would choose you over and over again if I could.

Love - Sandra

Nita McKinley

Dear Mom,

I've been reflecting on your incredible life journey, and I just wanted to express how deeply I admire your strength and sacrifice. Born during the Great Depression in 1929, in Vicksburg, Mississippi, and raised by your grandmother after your mother passed away, you've always had to carry a heavy weight. Your grandmother, born in 1897, was a remarkable woman herself, a Chickasaw Indian who escaped the horrors of slavery by using her gift of song on the Rivers of the Mississippi Showboat, and her resilience flows through you. I think about how, at 20 years old, you became a mother and managed to run a nightclub in Mississippi that supported you and your grandmother despite the fact that her mortgage was only five dollars. It still was a struggle to make ends meet. Yet you found a way to provide for the family and kept everything going. And even though you had your own dreams, you made the unselfish decision to give your younger sister the opportunity to attend Tougaloo University. You could have gone yourself because you were not only the first child but you too were smart, creative, and brilliant, but you put her education first, and that choice set her on an extraordinary path. Though she originally pursued law, she ultimately became a mathematician and made history. She became the first Black woman hired by California State Transportation (CALTRANS), and by challenging the Engineering State Test, she became the first Black woman Engineer and first Black woman to design freeways for CALTRANS, including the 105 freeway. Your path was just as inspiring. Mom, you were the last person in line eligible to cast a ballot when the announcement was made that Blacks no longer needed a ticket to vote.

When you moved to California in 1955, you were married, a housewife, and later became a mother to five more children. One of your children, me, was born with a heart disease, having five major and three minor open heart surgeries. The doctor said to the family, take her home and love on her because she won't live past twelve. You and the family loved on me and even spoiled me, and because of your dedication and love, I'm still here today at 66. You stayed home to take care of me and the rest of your children, yet you always managed to build a successful business at home after obtaining your beautician's license, so you could provide for us while being there for your family.

In 1969, you began working for the Los Angeles School District as a Paraprofessional Teacher's Assistant, where you remained for twenty-five years without ever missing a day's work until retiring. Students who you taught still admire and honor you to this day. Your work ethic and devotion were unmatched. Even outside of work, your talent shone through—Art Linkletter, part owner of Disneyland, loved your cooking so much he would beg you to come and cook for him.

Your life has been one of sacrifice, resilience, and love. I am so proud to have called you my mom and to be your child, and I am endlessly grateful for the legacy of strength, dedication, and warmth that you've passed down to me.

With Love and Deepest Admiration,
Nita McKinley

Sonya McDonald

Because of You

To My Beautiful Mom, My Guiding Light

As I sit down to write this, memories wash over me like the warm rays of the sun, each one a reflection of the countless ways you've brought love, light, and joy into my life. It's hard to capture all that you mean to me in a single letter, but I hope these moments can show you even a glimpse of how truly treasured you are.

I remember standing on my tiptoes in the kitchen, peering eagerly over the countertop as you poured the batter into a mixing bowl. My tiny hands would reach out for the beater, that sacred moment of licking the batter bringing pure delight, the sweetness of cake a symbol of all the sweetness you have added to my life. I didn't realize then that you were teaching me more than just baking; you were teaching me the joy of simple pleasures, the comfort found in small moments, and the gift of sharing happiness.

Christmas was always a time when your love for us overflowed, woven into every cookie, every ornament, every ribbon. The smell of cinnamon and sugar in the air as we decorated cookies together, my childish fingers smearing icing and sprinkles with wild excitement—you were always so patient, allowing me to express my creativity in the messiest ways. Your love was in every batch of cookies, every carefully chosen decoration. And in those moments, you were not just my mom; you were my best friend, my safe place.

Holidays were magical because of you. I think of the way you would transform our home with traditions and incredible food, cooking Thanksgiving meals from scratch, the air filled with delicious smells, all those flavors coming together with your love. It wasn't just during holidays either; you had an endless supply of snacks for us, always welcoming my friends over with food, warmth, and that special care you showed everyone. Your open heart and generosity taught me the value of kindness, of loving others through the smallest yet most meaningful ways.

I think of how you have shown that same deep love for your beautiful granddaughters from the very first day they entered the world. You were at the hospital, waiting to meet them, and I'll never forget the joy in your eyes as you held them for the first time. Those were some of the most precious moments, as you have showered them with love from the beginning and have continued to be there for them every step of the way. They're so blessed to have a Nana who loves them as much as you do.

You have also taught me, by example, the importance of self-care and self-love. I watched as you always took time to look your best, tending to your appearance with a care that instilled confidence in me. You showed me that it's not only okay to love and care for oneself but that it's an essential part of becoming a strong and confident woman. Through your example, I learned to take pride in myself and value my own well-being.

I'll never forget those days picking strawberries together in the field, when we'd eat so many that we'd both feel sick afterward, laughing about it later. And all the times we'd crack up over the littlest things until we were both in tears, laughing so hard it was impossible to stop. Those simple moments, full of laughter and love, are stitched into the fabric of who I am.

Your love, Mom, is like a garden that blooms in every season—nurtured with patience, always growing, and filled with care. You have guided me through each phase of life, from the spring of my childhood to the autumn of my hardest days, your love holding me steady through it all.

You have always had this magical way of knowing exactly what to say and when to say it. Through every joy and heartbreak, every high and low, you have been my steady anchor, my calm in the storm. In times when life felt overwhelming, your words would wrap around me like a soft blanket, offering comfort and peace. You taught me to stand tall, even when I felt like crumbling, to find beauty in the broken, and to always believe in myself, even when I had doubts.

You have been so much more than a mom to me. You have been my confidante, my biggest cheerleader, and my best friend. I look at my daughters and feel such gratitude that they have you in their lives. They, too, will grow up with a Nana who is always there to listen, to hug, to celebrate, and to console. They will grow up with the kind of love that has no boundaries, the kind of love that is patient, understanding, and unwavering. They will know what it means to be truly cherished because of you.

Every day, I want to remind you of how deeply I love and appreciate you. You are the heart of our family, the warmth that fills our lives, and the one who makes everything brighter. You are a gift from God, and I am beyond blessed to have you as my mom and my best friend. I am endlessly grateful for the gift of you, for every memory, every lesson, and every moment you have shared with me. I love you with all my heart. You are my best friend.

Thank you for being you. Thank you for being the best mom and Nana we could ever hope for. Thank you for teaching me to see the world with wonder, to face it with courage, and to walk through it with love.

For my one and only mom, I hope this letter is a small gift that expresses even a part of the immense love and gratitude I feel for you. You are, and always will be, my guiding light.

With all my love,
Sonya

Ciara Lewis

Dear Mom,

The last 35 years have been an amazing adventure. From birth on, you've always been my best friend, my rock, my joy, my peace, but most of all, my anchor. From diaper changes, kissing boo-boos, fun and games, tea parties, watching movies, wiping tears, middle school drama, my first boyfriend/crush, the stress of high school, the birth of my daughter, my health issues, surgeries and procedures, starting college, the extra stress in between, up until now you've been there every step of the way. You never let me fall, and if I did, you always picked me back up and helped me get back on my feet.

I just want you to know that all the discipline and talks paid off and have really helped me in life. Most importantly, they have helped me raise my daughter. I know you may have thought that I didn't listen or take heed to what you taught me, but trust me, I did. I came out hardheaded and stubborn, but in a good way. I'm thankful for all the lessons you taught me growing up; they have shaped me into the woman I am today.

I'm here to tell you, Mom, that without you, none of this would be possible. I would never have made it through my birth without you, I would never have been able to take that next step with being a mother, I would never have been able to stay strong and keep going or get through college, start my business, made it to one of the top entrepreneur programs OMBW, be a part of my first published #1 International Best Seller Anthologies, be in global magazines, made it in the *Forbes* magazine, and continuing on today. You gave me the light to find new and better paths in life, to not only help me but provide a better life and opportunities for my daughter. My world would be completely black and empty without you, there would be no color to see or light to shine, no good path to follow. You have been my Saving Grace.

Through every argument or disagreement we have ever had, I've taken something from each of them, but the thing that I have taken from it the most is being BLESSED to even be able to have a mother who cares enough about me to disagree and put me in my place when needed. Not everyone has that, and to some, that may sound crazy or not something to be thankful for. Disagreements and arguments can sometimes be the best thing for a relationship and help both parties grow for the better. Ever since we lost your mom, aka my granny, I feel that we have both grown and changed. We have become way better and closer, and I didn't think we could get any closer than we already were. I think we finally understood why she stayed on us about arguing and how it's not worth it all the time. I now see that we don't just disagree on every little thing now, we choose what matters, and now we learn and grow from each one.

I know a lot of people grieve so hard after losing their parents that they change or can't go on living life like before, but not you. You grieved, but you still stood strong and held on for me and your granddaughter. You never gave up and kept fighting through the pain and all. You even buttered yourself and made good choices for yourself after she passed. You took one of the hardest jobs and made it look like a walk in the park from an outside view, even though I know how rough it was and still is on you. I knew I had to show up for you more after that and that's what I've promised myself that I would do.

All my work and accomplishments are for you, and I want to share every bit of it with you. You will always be a part of my journey, Mom, no matter where I go or what I accomplish. At the end of it all, you're my true accomplishment. I wish I could truly express to you how much I love you and how much you mean to me, but the truth is there will not be enough words or actions to express it. You're the most amazing and strongest woman I know.

My life has been a joy just by having you by my side. I am so thankful for you. You make the tough roads easy, the frowns into smiles, the sadness into happiness, and most of all, you turn my cries into laughter. I wouldn't want to spend my life or share my joys with anyone other than you.

Thank you, Mom, for all you have done and all you do, but most of all, thank you for being you. You have supported me through every journey, even the rough ones, and have been my biggest fan. I love you, Mom!

Hunyah Irfan

Dear Mama,

For this holiday season, I would like to give you a camera. You have always been on my side for my projects, my work, and the adventures of you and me trying new things.

I want you to enjoy Christmas 2024 with us at Ali and Faria's house. We will play board games and drink some tea. We will sit and enjoy our time. We will watch as the snow is there and it's the holiday season.

Mama, I have been strong towards my goals because of your support. I have had struggles in the past. These were recovering from the accident and then learning how to walk again after an internal injury when I was 22. Also, finding a job was so hard for me, and we had limited resources, especially in Malton.

Mama, you always support me in what I want to do and every time I try something new. At one time, I did try for retail jobs because working in a store like Urban Planet, Forever 21, Ardene, Gap, and Old Navy looked so fun. But it was so competitive.

I remember those days when we started attending community events. I got to wear my party clothes to those events. It was so much fun, and I was recovering from an accident.

Mama, I know I might do food reviews because every weekend, you try new restaurants, attend community dinners, talk to the community, help others, listen to their stories, and also try new cuisines.

I know you put a lot of hard work into making me, Ali, and Virsa as independent as we are today. The three of us are able to look after the house and take care of ourselves when we have to.

Mama, you made three of us independent by not just looking after the house and taking care of ourselves:

1. Making us to be mature
2. To live in the moment
3. The importance of working
4. Being able to take the bus
5. Being able to help others
6. The importance of people, not things
7. To know the difference between hardworking and not hardworking
8. To run a business
9. To work as a community
10. To help people
11. To donate to those in need
12. To listen to people's stories
13. To have our own lives
14. To make good and responsible choices

Mama, it is surprising how people know your name in the community every time we go somewhere.

I try to make you happy in every way I can. Yes, I'm always working on my education because I know you let me grow further in my career.

Mama, I remember when I was a teen, you told me to go to community services. Now at 32 years old, I'm able to go to community services.

Mama, I know your goal is to connect people to their dreams. I know you like to see people meet their goals. I hope you let me reach my goals as well.

Mama, today with your support, I have achieved a lot.

I know in 2025, I will achieve more. There are bigger achievements I know I will get in the next year.

I know, Mama, you will also achieve something bigger than you are right now.

Mama, I can't talk to anyone else about my problems. Talking to you about my problems has always made me feel better.

Then, I know what to do and what steps to take.

Mama, I want to give you a new camera, so you have more memories to store.

Also, more photography of landscapes and seasons to do.

Mama, Ali, Virsa, and I want you to be happy.

That is why this holiday season, we want to sit and enjoy the best we can.

Mama, I know you came back from a trip. It was tiring. 14 hours to sit.

I know you have time to take a break from work and enjoy yourself by trying different restaurants, shopping, and going to our family and friends' places back home. I know you were still working even after your vacation started that day when you left for your trip.

Mama, I wanted to come and say bye.

I know we had the video call, but I wanted you to be back and have a good time with me, Ali, Virsa, and Faria.

Mama, I know you put a lot of hard work into everything.

This year, we want you to have a good time.

Because of your trips to Sweden, then to Vancouver, and now to Pakistan, Mama, I miss you a lot. I hope when you come back, you bring back memories and stories to share with us. I also want to have authentic chips from Pakistan.

Mama, we want to hear from you.

This Christmas, we will meet at Ali and Faria's house and talk.

Mama, I know you are the best person I can go to and discuss my stories.

I know I talk too much, but that is because every day, I have something new.

Although, Ali and Virsa don't talk that much.

I know I'm talkative but that is because I'm so similar to you.

Mama, I know 2024 was a good year.

Mama, I know 2025 is going to be better.

I miss you, and thank you.

Sincerely,
Hunyah Irfan

Julianne Williams

Dear Mom,

I have said many times I am so glad YOU are my mom.

You have sacrificed over and over for the sake of your children and grandchildren. This letter is my living tribute to you, so you know all you have done is appreciated and recognized.

There is never a time I don't feel like the most wanted daughter on this earth. Every day you lived out what you always said: "All I wanted was to be a mom". You have fiercely protected your family and set an example for all of us.

I tell my kids all the time what you used to tell my sister, brother, and me about siblings because you were right—when all else fails, you have to love your siblings. Since you were an "only child", it was important to you to give us siblings (even though sometimes you shake your head at what siblings do) so that we would always have someone by our side.

You have been so brave as our mother. Whether it was my heart issues or other things, you never gave up. Even when it was harder than hard, you found strength. Without that example, I don't think I would have made it this far. When I am feeling stressed or discouraged, I think back to a young mom making life-altering decisions for me, not knowing the outcome.

One of the sweetest things about you is how you constantly tell your kids and grandkids how special we are. According to you, there is no one on this planet who is as beautiful, handsome, smart, or thoughtful as us. While I'm certain we are special, I'm not certain we are THAT special. But when you are growing up, the unconditional and accepting love of those statements makes you feel extremely special and confident enough to go and chase your dreams. I know now that not everyone has continuous encouragement to take those risks to achieve big goals.

And, in my darkest times, you have always been a comfort and hope for me. I have cried so many tears at your kitchen table, over the phone late at night, and while trying to figure out how to parent on my own. No matter what, you listened. No matter what, you reassured. No matter what, you told me the truth. No matter what, I knew that somehow I was going to be OK, even if it wasn't easy. And I know when you were holding me up, you were sad with me and for me. I know you had a dream for all of us and worked so hard to help us achieve ours as well. I also know you will never give up or stop praying until you see things come to pass.

The most important legacy you will leave is the guarantee of eternal life for your children and grandchildren by leading us to Jesus. Your faith is so strong and inspiring. I'll never forget you taking notes in your Bible during church, devoting time to lead Bible study, and letting me wear your rings when we sat in church. I'm certain that is why I love jewelry so much!

You have always been a fun mom and one everyone wanted to be around. Even now at 81, you are still considered "cool" and fun by my friends. I don't have a lot of childhood memories at an early age, but I do remember you always having music playing, beads in our doorways, and sitting at the counter eating Mac and Cheese and calling it dynamite. Those macrame plant hangers you made, making your neck orange, were pretty groovy too.

Of course, we also won't forget the wooden spoon in your purse, the Vega, or Alpha Beta. Those fruit rolls were the best treat.

The stories of you and Dad are so funny. The fact that you believed that cows on a hill had legs of different lengths showed how much you loved and trusted him. You set a good example of a loving relationship as we were growing up, even if we were grossed out when Dad would come home, and you would kiss a little too much in the kitchen before he changed out of his suit.

I have cherished our trips to Armenia and our time together in church and Armenian School. You have blessed us by keeping our culture alive in our family. My love for cooking definitely came from learning how to cook traditional Armenian food with Ma, Gram, and you. I'm even happier that my kids love the food so much and are learning to make the dishes so they continue to be passed down. Of course, I know they like your cabbage dolma more than mine, but hopefully, I will be able to make it as well as you someday.

Last, I am so proud of your professional accomplishments. You placed your desires on hold to stay home and raise us. You have been a tireless advocate for children, and, through your work as a therapist, have helped so many find their path to a better life. Through this, you taught us to live our passion and to find an occupation that gave back to our community. And, on top of all of that, you volunteered endless hours to your church and the Ladies' Guild to ensure you were doing your part, so our church would continue for future generations.

Mom, your gracious and loving ways have been a beautiful precedent for me. I will work to conduct myself similarly. Thank you for all you have done to raise us to be good human beings. I hope you are proud of what I have done and become. I could have never accomplished any of it without you.

I love you and can't wait for more adventures,
Julianne

Stacey Dorenfeld

Dear Mom,

I wish you were still here. I miss you every single day, despite all the things you didn't get right. It's a strange feeling—to long for someone who hurt me, who failed to protect me, who couldn't see my needs. I miss you, but I don't miss the way you often overlooked me, and how my needs felt invisible. So many times, I needed you to step in, to protect me from harm, but you couldn't—or wouldn't. It took me a long time to understand that you were sick, fighting battles I couldn't see. I get it now, I really do, but that understanding doesn't erase the weight you left behind. Thinking of you still brings tears to my eyes.

I often wonder about you and the choices you made. How could you let those things happen to me? Were you lost in your own mind, trying to escape from a life you didn't want? Were you searching for something that no one could provide? It felt like you were always seeking something other than me and my brother. It was your job to protect us, but you threw us to the wolves. And sometimes, you were one of those wolves too. That's the hardest part—you were both the danger and the one I loved the most. It's such a conflict to hold inside, but I never stopped loving you, even after everything.

I still remember the time we made chocolate chip cookies together. Just one simple day, but it's a moment I cling to. For those hours, you were all mine. You weren't distracted or angry; you were just there, with me. That small slice of time, less than a couple of hours, remains in my heart even now, 55 years later. I hold onto it because it was one of the few times I saw the mother I desperately wished you could be. Those are the moments I wanted more of—the mother who laughed with me, who made me feel safe and cherished.

Instead, you were often lost in your own pain and addiction, a world I couldn't understand.

When you overdosed for the last time, I wondered if you truly wanted to leave this world or if you just wanted to disappear for a while. The thought still haunts me. Why did you have to relapse? Seeing the words "suicide" on your death certificate felt like a punch to my soul. The pain of your decision became mine to bear. I know life was hard for you; I've come to understand that more with time. But your absence made my path so much harder. You always said it was my brother who needed your concern, that he was the one to worry about. I can still hear you saying it. You never thought I needed anything, that I could handle it all on my own. Was I really that strong, even as a little girl? Or were you just too consumed by your own pain to see mine? The abuse I endured was overwhelming, and it still haunts me. I wonder if you knew the depth of it and chose to look away, or if facing it was simply too much for you.

Taking care of my brother, with his mental illness and addiction, has been a burden I was never meant to carry. You made him an addict, you made him troubled—through your own abuse and the abuse you allowed. It became my responsibility, and I had no say in it. You chose to bring us into this world, and when you left, you abandoned everything you couldn't handle. It wasn't fair then, and it doesn't feel fair now. There are days when I'm angry at you for putting everything on me without a second thought. Yet, even with all that, I still ache for you. I still long for the mother I needed you to be, the mother I believe you could have been if life had been kinder. My tears flow as I write this.

It's been 38 years since you took your life, but it feels like it was just yesterday. The shock of it, the finality of your decision—it's something I've never fully processed. People say time heals all wounds, but I'm not sure that's true. The memory of losing you feels fresh, as if no time has passed at all. It forces me to confront all the grief I've tried to bury, the longing that still sits quietly inside me. It brings back both the love and the pain.

I wanted to say something I've never been able to say out loud: I forgive you. I know you were suffering. I know you faced things I could never fully understand and that you did the best you could with what you had. It's taken me a long time to reach this place—a place where I can let go of the anger and resentment. I've realized that holding onto that anger only hurts me more. I've had to learn how to make peace with everything you couldn't be, to accept the mother I had instead of the mother I dreamed of.

I hope that wherever you are, you've found some peace. I pray that you are no longer haunted by the things that tormented you in life. I pray you've been able to heal in ways you couldn't when you were here. I like to imagine that you're watching over me, that you see the struggles I've faced and the strength I've had to find within myself. I hope you're proud of me, even if you never told me that when you were alive.

And I hope that someday, somewhere, I'll see you again. I don't know what happens after we leave this world, but if there's a chance that we can meet again, I'd like to believe we could heal together. I'd like to believe we could find the love that was lost between us, and that maybe, for the first time, we could both be at peace. Until then, I'll hold onto the good memories, however few they might be, and I'll keep forgiving you, day by day.

With all my love, and all the pieces of my broken heart,

Your Daughter
Stacey Dorenfeld

Lovely LaGuerre

A Daughter's Letter to Her Beloved Mother

Dear Mom,

Where do I even begin?

I feel like my heart is brimming with emotions that words can hardly contain. I'm hoping this letter will articulate the love and gratitude I carry for you, my dearest mother, my best friend, my queen.

My heart is overflowing with so much love, gratitude, and admiration. Yet, I want to capture everything that you mean to me. First, thank you for giving me life, and I want to share a glimpse of the immense impact you've had on my life. You're more than just my mother. You are my confidante, my greatest supporter, my voice of reason, and the brightest example of strength and resilience I have ever known.

I am so profoundly grateful to call you "Mom!"

Every day, I realize how truly lucky I am to have a mother like you. Someone who has not only nurtured me but has also shown me the beauty in life, the joy in the little things, and the importance of kindness toward others. You've shown me what it means to live fully, to laugh wholeheartedly, and to love deeply.

Growing up, I was in awe of the way you cared for our family and everyone around you. You have a heart that is as big as the sky, filled with compassion and generosity that knows no bounds. You're one of those rare individuals who can truly see the best in everyone. Observing you over the years, the way you touch lives simply by being you has taught me so much about kindness and empathy. You've given me an example to strive for more with purpose, and it's one I will always carry with me.

One of the most beautiful gifts you've given me is our shared history.

When you shared with me about our family's journey, our roots, our values, and the challenges we've overcome, it became clear to me how much strength and courage runs in our blood. Those stories, the resilience and faith passed down through generations, have shaped me. They remind me to hold my head high and to face life with dignity and grace. You always told me that our values are what define us, and you lived that truth every single day. In so many ways, you were not just teaching me about our heritage; you were teaching me how to live.

Thank you for being my brightest star and such a wonderful role model. Watching you pursue your goals with determination and grace has shown me that no dream is too big. You have this incredible zest for life, an unstoppable drive to achieve, and a quiet strength that has never wavered. Your resilience and determination have inspired me more than I can say. You've shown me that a woman can be strong and gentle, assertive and caring, driven and compassionate, all at once. Every time I face a challenge, I think of you, of all you've overcome, and I find the strength to keep going.

Mom, you have always been my greatest cheerleader and always will be. I can't count the times I came to you for advice, worried or unsure, and you lifted me up with your words of encouragement. You believed in me even when I didn't believe in myself. You've been there through every triumph and every stumble, celebrating my victories and helping me learn from my mistakes. I am so proud to have a mother who always stood by me, no matter what. I know that not everyone is blessed with this kind of unconditional love, and I cherish it with all my heart.

More than anything, you are my best friend. With you, I can be completely myself. We laugh together, we share our hopes and dreams, and sometimes we simply sit in silence, knowing that words aren't necessary. Our bond is something precious, something I carry with me everywhere I go. Your wisdom, your humor, and your kindness are woven into the fabric of who I am. You've taught me that friendship isn't just found outside the family; it can exist right within, in the person who knows you best and loves you most.

Your brilliance amazes me every single day. Your mind is a treasure, filled with so much insight, knowledge, and understanding. I have always admired your wisdom, how you see the world with such clarity, and how you can see all sides of a situation and bring a fresh perspective to even the most complex issues. I've learned so much just from watching you think, and from observing the way you approach life's challenges with a calm, thoughtful, and balanced mindset. I know I'll carry your wisdom with me always, and I'll do my best to pass it on to the generations that come after me.

Throughout my life journey, I have realized more and more how much you've shaped who I am. You are my inspiration, my queen, and my role model. Your values are the foundation of my life, and your love is my guiding light. Everything good in me is a reflection of you, and I will forever be grateful for that.

I want to say thank you, Mom. Thank you for every sacrifice you made, big and small. Thank you for your patience, for your gentle guidance, and for giving me the freedom to find my own path while always being there to support me. Thank you for teaching me to be strong and independent, to pursue my dreams, and to live life with purpose and passion. Most of all, thank you for simply being you—for being the kind, loving, inspiring woman who raised me and who continues to shape my life in more ways than you could ever know.

I can't imagine a life without you. The thought of it makes me realize even more how precious every moment with you truly is. I promise to cherish every single one, to honor you with my actions, and to carry on the legacy of love, kindness, and strength that you have built. I am so incredibly blessed to be your daughter, and to have the privilege of learning from you and loving you every day.

Thank you for being my mother, my best friend, my biggest supporter, and my forever role model. I am so grateful for every moment, every lesson, and every memory we've shared. You are my heart, my hero, my home, and my forever brightest light!

With all my love, always and forever.

Your Daughter,
Lovely LaGuerre

Astrid Boot

Dear Mum,

If you had told me years ago, I would write this letter from my heart to yours, I would definitely not have believed it, but now the whole world may read this. It is a letter about how our relationship has transformed in 54 years into a great relationship where we feel connected, more aligned, and a warm love.

When I was little, you were always working hard with Dad to have a successful business at home so there would be food on the table. You had many tasks, from raising three children, cooking, cleaning, and sewing clothes, to running a shop with household items, filling up tractors' tanks at the diesel pump, bookkeeping, doing administration and HR for the business, delivering and picking up parts for the business, hosting gatherings and shows, and advising and making decisions with Dad about the business. You were indispensable!

One day, Dad, my two sisters, and I came back home with a puppy; it became your fourth child to raise, even though the puppy wasn't your idea. This dog became your companion and shadow; wherever you went, he followed you. You've also raised several cats and kittens over the years.

I've worked hard to achieve the best possible results at school, and you've noticed this, even though you didn't mention it. You made our lunch every morning to take to school and drank a cuppa every afternoon when we came home. When it snowed, you came to pick me up with the big van and kids from our village went with their pushbikes with us to be dropped home.

You always came to watch me perform when I played musical instruments, and with dancing and gymnastics performances, where Dad stopped going. It felt special that you took that time for me.

On many occasions, my younger sister and I had disagreements that became a fight when I felt not taken into account. It must have been frustrating for you to witness. For me, it felt that you favoured my younger pretty sister, which decreased my confidence and self-esteem. When I decided at 21 to move out as a solution, you helped me to turn my new place into a cosy one.

After my daughter was born, I noticed that when you visited me feeling down, you left after an hour feeling happier and lighter, leaving me behind feeling down. In the end I couldn't make another decision than to end our contact. I had to sort out how I could stay in my own energy and power and how to protect my boundaries. It must have been hard for you, but it has also brought us so much!

You've learned about boundaries, feeling inside yourself if something feels good for you, and acting upon that. You're reading a book about being highly sensitive, and you recognise so much about yourself in it. It's great to see how you're learning more about yourself.

Last year, you found out that you've been carrying trauma with you from losing your dad when you were young. You didn't have a warm and loving mother, and you didn't experience a pleasant youth. I've carefully offered to help you through my healing work, and you grabbed my offer with both hands, to my surprise. I felt honoured to be able to help you and saw you enthusiastically giving me feedback about the positive changes you noticed happening. You became more in tune with your Self and your feelings. Your mind and heart got more connected. The chaotic stressed energy that my sisters and I always sensed around you transformed into a calmer energy.

You're on your path of learning to let go of needing to be in control and to accept the boundaries of others. You've shared with me how challenging it is as a mother to watch my younger sister struggle with health issues and overwhelm and not have to do anything. You are a giver to people in need. You are a blessing to them because you're an organiser, a logical thinker, and an action taker. Exactly what people can use in a devastating time. You can take over responsibilities so that they can focus on their feelings, while things like their household continue to run smoothly.

For an 80-year-old, you are incredibly fit! I'm sure many admire you for that. You cycle when it's good weather so you can leave the car at home. You play tennis several times a week. You've started yoga and noticed its positive benefits. I believe this is amazing, and I am proud of you.

I am proud of the woman you have become. I forgive you for everything that has happened. I know you've done the best with what you knew at the time. You are a very strong and resilient woman, and it is totally fine to prioritise yourself and your needs. You've worked hard in your life, and you may now relax and enjoy life fully. That's what you deserve.

This year, you've helped me tremendously. You felt I could use help when my daughter moved out, and I had to let her go. You understood, and I felt supported. It is absolutely amazing how we've come to now have a loving relationship as mother and daughter. Your love feels warm now because you've opened your heart. I live on the other side of the world and haven't seen you for 5 years, but next time, I'll give you a hug, and I will need to cry.

For the first time, I've sent you a Mother's Day card because the words 'I love you' finally resonated deeply. You thanked me for the card, and I could feel my message on it had touched your heart.

We now have a healed foundation for love. I love you and am thankful you are my mother because, thanks to you, I've become who I am today.

With love,
Astrid

Jennifer Payeur

To My Beautiful Mother, Carol,

As I reflect on our journey together in this life, I'm overwhelmed by the richness of our shared experiences. Each memory is a thread in the beautiful tapestry of our relationship, woven with love, laughter, respect, challenges, and sometimes tears.

From the moment you held me in your arms, our souls intertwined in a dance of love, challenge, and growth. Two fire signs, often with opposing views, and yet we grew to understand and love each other despite those differences.

Your unwavering support has been the cornerstone of my existence, shaping me into the woman I am today. Through every triumph and tribulation, you've stood beside me, a beacon of strength and wisdom. Your life story is a testament to the power of resilience. You've faced adversity with grace, teaching me that true strength lies not in avoiding hardship, but in learning and rising above it. I've watched you transform obstacles into opportunities, pain into purpose, and fear into faith. Your ability to find light in the darkest of times has been my guiding star, a trait that has given me life in so many ways.

Even when we disagreed, your love never wavered. You taught me that love isn't just a feeling, but a choice – a daily commitment to support, nurture, and accept. This lesson has rippled through my relationships, enriching my connections with my husband, my children, and those around me.

Your journey of self-discovery and personal growth has been nothing short of miraculous. By doing your inner work, you've not only transformed your own life but have also paved the way for me, my children, and their children. The healing you've initiated in our family line is a gift that continues to unfold. What a blessing it has been to see this come to life in our extended family!

With strength, grace, courage, and determination, you broke free from generational patterns that no longer served. Your willingness to face your own shadows allowed light to pour into our family tree, illuminating new possibilities for growth and happiness. Because of your bravery, my children have inherited a legacy of emotional intelligence, expanded consciousness, self-awareness, compassion for others, and kindness. I know you understand the significance of this!

Your unwavering faith has also been a cornerstone of our family. In times of uncertainty, your trust in a higher power has been our anchor. You've shown me that faith isn't just about believing in good times, but about holding onto hope when the world seems dark. This teaching is a huge piece of your legacy and has changed the course of my life.

Together, we've faced challenges that seemed insurmountable. Yet, with your steadfast belief and our combined strength, we've moved mountains. From serious health scares to personal setbacks, your faith has been our foundation, propelling us forward when we were deep into the unknown.

The trust you've placed in God, in the goodness of people, and in the power of love has shaped my worldview. You've taught me to approach life with an open heart and to trust in the journey even when the destination is unclear. This legacy of trust is a gift I carry in my heart and soul.

Your role as a teacher has extended far beyond the classroom. Every day, in countless ways, you've continued to educate and inspire those around you, even when you had trouble speaking. Your lessons are woven into the fabric of my being, guiding my choices and shaping my character every single day.

Your curiosity about the world, your willingness to challenge your own beliefs, and your openness to new ideas are qualities I admire deeply. You've taught me that true wisdom comes not from knowing all the answers, but from always being willing to ask questions, and then to be quiet and listen.

One of the greatest gifts you've given me is the courage to speak my truth. You've encouraged me to stand up for what I believe in, even when it's unpopular or misunderstood. This lesson in authenticity has been invaluable, shaping my path and allowing me to live a life true to myself.

I cherish the simple moments we've shared – the quiet conversations, the laughter-filled family gatherings, the comforting hugs when words weren't enough. These moments have become the foundation of our bond. You've passed the importance of family onto me, something I didn't appreciate until I had my own children. And now, your beloved granddaughter, Katie, is continuing this beautiful legacy of family.

Even in our most difficult times, when misunderstandings or hurt feelings created distance between us, your love remained constant. Our ability to work through these challenges, to forgive, and to grow closer, has only strengthened our connection.

As our roles shift, with me now caring for you as you once cared for me, I'm struck by the beautiful circularity of life. In this phase of our journey together, I find myself filled with a deep sense of gratitude and a great love in my heart. For every sacrifice you made, for every lesson you taught, for every dream you encouraged – thank you. Your love has been the greatest gift of my life.

As we navigate this difficult transition, know that your legacy lives on in me, in my children, and in all the lives you've touched. I promise to carry forward your teachings, your strength, and your love. Your spirit will continue to guide and inspire many, a bright light showing the way.

Mom, you are more than just my mother – you are my teacher, my friend, my love, and my compass. The love between us transcends this lifetime, a bond that will endure beyond time and space. As you prepare for your next great adventure, know that you are loved beyond measure, cherished beyond words, and that your impact on this world is everlasting.

May you fly with the butterflies!

With all my love and gratitude,
Your daughter, Jennifer

Shirley Catalano

Dear Mom,

I'm so blessed that God chose me to be one of your many unique children. As I write you this letter, I am reminded of many wonderful memories we've shared over the years. I remember when I was a kid knowing that you were the prettiest mom and that I was your child. Although, Connie tried to make me believe that I was adopted. I was your 'mini me,' and I absolutely loved that you brushed my long hair (only when we didn't have to be somewhere, ouch) or that you rubbed my head. You watched all of the plays my siblings and friends made up and put on for you graciously! You listened to every new song I made up. Those childhood memories of you strutting your stuff as the classroom mom were pure gold. I mean, who wouldn't want to show off a rockstar like you to their friends? However, I knew that you were not afraid to be my mother, put your foot down when you needed to teach me right from wrong, to make sure I did my best. My younger years saw you suffer challenges that no one should ever have had to endure. Through them, you learned strength and determination to be able to push through. I admire your spunk, you are one the strongest people I know, and I am so lucky to have you as my mom. Even when times for you are tough, you keep going and never give up. I watched you kick cancer's butt through the love and grace of God. You took a risk at being an entrepreneur and ran a successful business.

You always let me know you were a mom who cared about me, loved me, and was there for me, no matter what. Especially after my accident, when you had to drive me daily to different outpatient therapies. Growing up with that kind of love and support made such a difference, it's a part of who I am today. Mom, you were never afraid to voice your opinion or be one to mince words, to put it lightly. I kept you guessing, didn't I? Especially, when you had other children running in many other directions. I know it wasn't easy for you and you did what you had to do. You always seemed ready for the next plot twist! Through all of our ups and downs, you faced challenges with the grace of a queen, pushing through with style. Even during those teenage tornado years when we didn't see eye to eye, we hung in there like champs.

Your impact on our family is like a masterclass in commitment and life lessons!

You hold onto hope that Jesus' healing touch is manifested in you. Mom, the testimonies that you shared will inspire and bless many others. Merry Christmas, Mom! God bless you always, and I love you lots, Beautiful!

Love,
Shirley Marie

A Letter to My... Daughter

Ciara Lewis

Dear Baby Girl,

Wow, what a wonderful journey it has been watching you grow. The day you were born was the happiest day of my life. My body was running with every emotion inside of me. I never knew that holding another human being that I grew up inside of me would bring so many different emotions and feelings all at once. I can't even explain the joy that came over me that day. I just knew when they placed you in my arms, I wanted to do everything possible to make you happy and protect you from that day forward. The scariest part was, I knew that I could no longer protect you like I could when you were in the womb, now that you were out in the world. So, my first way of protecting you was saying a PRAYER over you before you were born and after. I knew that form of protection would remain over you for life, no matter what the situation and when I couldn't be there.

When you came into this world, I knew then I could accomplish anything I wanted to. You gave me a new light of hope and strength, like Super Woman, to conquer whatever was thrown my way. There was a new reason to become more in life and do better, to make a straight path for you to walk when it was time. I was young when I had you, and at first, I was scared and questioned whether I was doing the right thing or not. However, I prayed and knew that it was meant for me to give birth to you and raise you. I was prepared to give up anything I had to, to become your mother. Most importantly, I knew I most definitely still had to get my education to be a good mother for you and provide for you.

I enjoyed every second of raising you, even on the toughest days, because I knew we would get through it together. On the toughest days, you would just look at me and smile and hug me with your tiny little arms.

My whole world would be made complete all over again. We would play for hours, making up our own games and rules: we would chase each other around the house, stay up late watching movies or playing games, eat our favorite snacks, go through all your toys, play dress up, sing, and our favorite thing, dance together. We would move the coffee table in the living room and just dance our hearts out. We spent several nights hanging out in my room because you just thought it was the coolest thing ever. Some days, you would bring your toys to my room while I did my schoolwork.

As you got older, things became a little more difficult, and we became a little distant. A lot of that was due to me having to play the good cop and bad cop. I couldn't be the cool mom/best friend all the time, and I had to start disciplining more. You didn't like that too well, but it had to be done. It broke my heart when that time came because I could remember all the times when we were so close and how you used to cry for me or always wanted to know where I was going or what I was doing. I knew as time went on, we would find our way back and be close again.

I can say watching you grow up has been the most amazing thing, and I would do it all over again in a heartbeat. You went from being this little sweet, sassy girl to a little girl who then became stuck in her shell because she was scared to let her true potential show, to this young teen who found herself and was ready to let people know who she was, to now a young woman who has done a complete 360 and come completely out of her shell. You made a huge decision almost 2 years ago to move to a bigger city, leaving all your friends and finishing high school at a new school. You started going to the gym on your own, meeting new friends, working, going to Church on your own, driving, planning a life for yourself, and having the opportunity to graduate early in December. It's an understatement to say how proud I am of you and how proud I am to be your mother. You are beautiful inside and out and have made every second worth living for. I look forward to continuing to watch you grow and see what you do next.

You are my inspiration and everything I have done and do, I do it all for you. It's because of you that I am who I am today and have had the courage that I did to get where I am. You have shown me the true meaning of love, patience, kindness, and what is worth fighting for. You have shown me why I can't give up and, when I lose my strength, exactly where to find it. You're the colorful rainbow in my world and the light at the end of my tunnel. You're my heart, and what keeps me going every day I get up. If I ever lost you, it would be like losing my lungs and having no oxygen to breathe.

Keep shining, baby girl, and remember I'll always be right here beside you every step of the way. I will always be your biggest fan. Thank you for letting me be your mom and for loving me for who I am. Most of all, thank you for being you.

Love always! Mom

Lovely LaGuerre

A Mother's Letter to Her Beloved Daughters

To My Precious Daughters,

From the moment I first held each of you in my arms, I knew I was holding my whole world. Even then, before I knew your personalities, your dreams, or the paths your lives would take, I knew one thing for certain: I was blessed beyond words to be your mother. Watching you both grow, evolve, and come into your own has been the most extraordinary journey of my life.

As I pour my thoughts into writing this small letter to you both, I find myself reflecting on all the moments we've shared moments that might seem ordinary, yet to me, are filled with extraordinary love and gratitude. I am in awe of what you are becoming. You girls are wise beyond your years, thoughtful, compassionate, and endlessly curious in your own ways. It's a rare gift to know who you are and what you want and yet, here you both stand so confident, so sure, with a light in your eyes that tells me you're ready to take on the world.

You both are, and always will be, the brightest light in my life. Every day with you is a gift, and being your mother is a privilege that fills my heart beyond measure. To think that I am lucky enough to witness the people you are becoming—the kindness, strength, and wisdom you each possess—is truly the greatest blessing. I am in awe of you both.

My dearest Ebony, it moves me deeply to see how you care for others. I've watched you extend kindness and empathy to others around you, and I can't tell you how proud it makes me. In a world that sometimes feels cold, you have warmth. In a world that can be unkind, you have a gentleness and positivity that I know will serve as a beacon for anyone lucky enough to know you. You bring hope, kindness, and strength to those around you, and watching you spread light in this way is one of my greatest joys.

My sweet princess Ari, we've shared countless beautiful conversations late nights in the kitchen, mornings over coffee, and fun and quiet car rides when words seem to flow effortlessly. I cherish these moments more than you know. You ask thoughtful questions, you listen, and you hold a perspective on life that is rare and beautiful. You dream big, and you chase those dreams with purpose and resilience. I can't begin to express how inspiring and privileged it is to witness those monumental moments and experiences along your sides.

To see you, and how you view life with such clarity, vibrancy, and purpose, is astounding. I marvel at the strength and wisdom you both possess; it is as though the universe has given me not just daughters but lifelong friends and teachers. You have taught me to see the world through fresh eyes, to approach each day with gratitude, and to embrace life's uncertainties with grace and courage.

Your minds, oh, how brilliant they are! You have this unquenchable thirst for knowledge, for growth, for self-discovery. The way you see the world, the way you challenge it, and the way you strive to understand is remarkable to me. You are thinkers, doers, and creators in ways I could never have imagined, and I am forever humbled by your brilliance. It is a gift not only to me but to the world, and I am endlessly excited to see where it will take you both.

There's something deeply comforting in knowing that you will carry this love, this strength, and this wisdom into the lives of others. I know, beyond a shadow of a doubt, that you are destined for greatness. You are my brightest shining stars, and there is no limit to what you can accomplish. I do not doubt that the stars are aligning for you and that whatever path you choose, will be marked by your remarkable spirit, resilience, and kindness with the Lord's grace.

Every day, I am filled with gratitude to be part of your life. It is a blessing I don't take for granted, and I cherish every moment—both the monumental and the seemingly small. You've given my life a depth, purpose, and meaning that words can hardly capture, and for that, I will forever be grateful. I am here to support you, to cheer for you, and to love you fiercely and unconditionally through every step of your journey.

As you both step forward into the future, know that my undying love is with you always. It's a love that is timeless, unwavering, and boundless. My hope for you is that you will continue to chase your dreams with the same courage and passion that you show now. You will find joy in the journey, strength in the challenges, and peace in knowing that you are profoundly loved.

Thank you for being my daughters. Thank you for being my brightest light. Thank you for filling my life with love, laughter, and purpose. I can't imagine a world without you in it, nor would I ever want to. You are my heart, my soul, and my everything.

With All my Love to my Outstanding Beautiful Daughters.

Love,
Mom

Idaliz Romero

A Letter to My Daughter

Hi Sweetie,

There are so many things I would like to write but this letter does not have enough room. Your presence changed my life in so many ways that it is impossible for me to express it all in this letter.

As a young girl, I had made the decision not to marry or have children. My childhood was not the best role model in that regard, but then I met your father, and he was the total opposite of what I had seen in my life, we were married 6 months later. When I first felt that I was expecting, I had my doubts, so I did what every young mom did—go visit the doctor. He notified me that I was not expecting and prescribed a medication. Only a week later, to tell me that I was expecting my first child. The doctor then realized his mistake, and he decided that I had to have an abortion. He insisted, but because I was adamant about not following his advice, he asked to speak to your father. We both agreed on my decision. Supposedly there would be some complications that may arise from the medication. I was willing to take that chance, and I am so grateful that I did because I received the most beautiful gift, YOU. Your father named you Linda, which in Spanish means pretty, and it was and still is the perfect name for you.

I had a connection with you since before you were born (no one believed me, of course). I knew you were going to be a girl because I saw you in my dream dressed in a red and white dress with beautiful green eyes. Everyone insisted that it was a boy, but my heart knew better. Your dad wanted a little girl and was disappointed with everyone's comments. When you were born, we asked the doctor, and when she said that you were a girl, I started telling my husband, "See, I told you so."

You were the most precious gift in my life, but of course, my upbringing influenced what kind of mother I would be. The fear that my marriage and motherhood would be like the others in my life scared me so much. Being abandoned by my parents and being told that I would be just like them was always in the back of my head. I struggled to be the best mom that I could be with what little I knew or missing role models about being a mom. I learned to be a mom by being your mom. I also learned about the traumas that were still inside me. I will never forget the day when those traumas reared their ugly head. You were three years old, and I just had given birth to your baby brother. I was exhausted and recovering (no excuses) when you behaved as a three-year-old would. My heart still aches from the memories of that day when with anger, I laid a hand on you. I went blind with rage, that now as I look back, had no logic. My husband walked in at that moment and yelled at me. I seriously did not hear him come. I snapped out of what seemed like a trance, and the impact of what I was doing hit me like a ton of bricks. I saw your beautiful face filled with tears and your questioning eyes, and I burst into tears. I held you in my arms while sitting on the floor, rocking both of us. I had never felt so much pain as I felt at that moment. I held you so tight, and right at that moment, I made a promise that I would never, ever lay a hand on you or your brother, and I kept it. I am so sorry that you had to experience some of what I have grown up with. You changed the cycle of abuse that I knew.

You are now a grown woman with children of your own, and I hope that I was a good role model for you as a mom. You were given challenges that I did not have to face. Your son (grandma's angel) was severely autistic, which took a toll on you and your family, making it so difficult to take care of my granddaughters. But you were strong and handled everything with love and understanding, especially with my grandson. Then life gave you another test when he was diagnosed with leukemia, and he passed away. I was in awe of your strength and courage as you faced the most difficult time of your life. I cannot say that I understand the pain you experienced, but I do understand the pain of seeing your broken heart. Thank you for giving me the opportunity to hold you and comfort you when you needed me most. I could not be prouder of the daughter, wife, and mom that you have become.

There is so much that I would like to say, but I want to end this letter by letting you know that I have been blessed to have you as my daughter. I am so grateful for the relationship we have and for our Family Fridays, where we talk, laugh, and spend time as a family. I want you to know that for as long as I am alive, I will be here for you. Thank you for being my daughter and my best friend. Thank you for the gift of making me a mom and a grandma. I love you more than you'll ever know. Remember that no matter where I am, I will always be a phone call away. Thank you again for being one of my greatest gifts! Always remember our song, "I like for always, I love you forever, as long as I am living, my baby you will be."

Love always
Mom

Anthea Siow

A Letter To My Daughter...
Jessica Karatasoulis – Siow

My Darling Dearest Daughter,

The day I brought you home when you were four months old, the love I felt for you was unconditional. You were not a foster child, but you were my daughter.

Having a daughter like you has brought so much joy to my life. You are one of a kind. I have never known a baby of four months old so determined to sit up on your own. By two years old, you had to button your own clothes, and by three years old, you tied your own shoe laces. I knew then that my precious daughter was determined, strong willed and independent.

Every time you cried, your dark brown eyes glistened like crystals. It would break my heart and make me want to protect you from anything that would make you sad and cry.

You don't hold grudges, and you don't stay angry, another quality of yours I admire.

I love how you have a way of finding humour in everything...you are the brightest shining star I have ever seen; you light up the darkest days with your beautiful smile and laughter.

Being independent is a wonderful quality, to be as strong willed as you can guide you well as you grow up. But remember to be patient, flexible and open to possibilities. Don't let your strong will and independence close you to all possibilities in life.

My daughter, remember to always love with all your heart, be kind, empathetic and compassionate to everyone you cross paths with.

Remember that even if I am not with you every day, it does not mean I don't cherish you or have you in my heart. I love you more than life itself.

Always be your authentic self, trust and love the person you are, dance to your own tune, laugh like there is no tomorrow, forgive those who hurt you, and always have people in your life who reciprocate the friendship.

You don't need to change for anyone, only for yourself.

Thank you for being my ray of sunshine. Without you, my world would be darker. You have touched my heart in so many ways my darling girl.

I am not always the best mum, or the mum you need me to be because I'm not there physically with you at home, but you are with me every minute of every day in my heart.

I love you to the moon and back.

All my love Mum. xxx

A Letter to my... Best Friend

Anthea Siow

To My Best Friend, John Ross Gardner.

Dearest John,

This is from me to you...my best friend...

I am imperfect, always have been, and always will be. You have never judged but accepted me for who I am. All that I am.

A friend like you is rare to find. You have seen me through the very low points of my life, from when Ky moved out the first time to my mental health diagnosis when my father passed away, and you have seen me through many dark moments. What I most love and appreciate is that you have always been in my corner, encouraging me to keep going, even when I couldn't see a tomorrow.

I love how we can laugh at ourselves and poke fun at one another while knowing it is a safe space. You are my nursery buddy, and no one else can take your place. It is never the same when I go on my own because you are not there for me to compete for the same best-looking plant we both want.

I feel I have known you for a lifetime, although it's only been ten years. Time has no bearing I realise when our friendship is one, I cherish it from the very first day I met you.

You have heard me like no one else ever has, you encouraged me when no one else did, and you gave me the right amount of guidance when I needed it the most. You were my family when I didn't have one of my own. For this, I am grateful, and I will never forget.

You are my best friend, but also like a brother.

You have been my lighthouse.

Showing the way when I am lost.

You show me the way back on track and keep me grounded.

You know all my secrets, and yet, you accept me for me, you love me just the way I am, warts and all.

Sometimes, I ask for too much or want what is not possible, but you never let me get away with it. That's what true friends do... you don't take my nonsense, and you challenge my maladaptive thoughts... all the time with empathy and compassion with a big serve of humour.

I love you, John, and I am so happy to see you happy. You and Brandon are perfect.

You will always be in my heart for a whole lifetime.

When the day comes for me to fly with the Angels or cook up a BBQ in hell, I will always remember you, our friendship, and the many, many fond memories I have of us.

With love,
Anthea

JOIN THE MOVEMENT!
#BAUW

Becoming An Unstoppable Woman
With She Rises Studios

She Rises Studios was founded by Hanna Olivas and Adriana Luna Carlos, the mother-daughter duo, in mid-2020 as they saw a need to help empower women worldwide. They are the podcast hosts of the *She Rises Studios Podcast* and Amazon best-selling authors and motivational speakers who travel the world. Hanna and Adriana are the movement creators of #BAUW - Becoming An Unstoppable Woman: The movement has been created to universally impact women of all ages, at whatever stage of life, to overcome insecurities, and adversities, and develop an unstoppable mindset. She Rises Studios educates, celebrates, and empowers women globally.

Looking to Join Us in our Next Anthology or Publish YOUR Own?

She Rises Studios Publishing offers full-service publishing, marketing, book tour, and campaign services. For more information, contact info@sherisesstudios.com

We are always looking for women who want to share their stories and expertise and feature their businesses on our podcasts, in our books, and in our magazines.

SEE WHAT WE DO

OUR PODCAST

OUR BOOKS

OUR SERVICES

Be featured in the Becoming An Unstoppable Woman magazine, published in 13 countries and sold in all major retailers. Get the visibility you need to LEVEL UP in your business!

Have your own TV show streamed across major platforms like Roku TV, Amazon Fire Stick, Apple TV and more!

Learn to leverage your expertise. Build your online presence and grow your audience with FENIX TV.
https://fenixtv.sherisesstudios.com/

Visit www.SheRisesStudios.com to see how YOU can join the #BAUW movement and help your community to achieve the UNSTOPPABLE mindset.

Have you checked out the *She Rises Studios Podcast?*

Find us on all MAJOR platforms: Spotify, IHeartRadio, Apple Podcasts, Google Podcasts, etc.

Looking to become a sponsor or build a partnership?

Email us at info@sherisesstudios.com

www.ingramcontent.com/pod-product-compliance
Lightning Source LLC
Chambersburg PA
CBHW050249010526
44107CB00003B/253